Living in the Dark Shadow of Opinion

Maurice Collis

DEDICATION

Thanks to my wife, Lidia, who encouraged me to write this. Thanks also to Hywel Simons who gave me sound advice and also to Dr Fida Afiouni who invited me to work with her students at the American University of Beirut on this project. They are Farah Itani, Ghina Al Shaal, Hala Halaby, Lara Saba, Reem Kambris, Natalie Maalouf, Mariam Chehab, Nora Dajani. The cover design is from Tanya Bizri

CONTENTS

ACKNOWLEDGMENTS

My thanks to the following authors and speakers. I have drawn on their thoughts in writing this dramatic workshop.

Dave Ulrich and Wayne Brock Bank – the HR Value proposition

Marcus Buckingham – First Break All the Rules

Gareth Jones and Rob Goffee – Why Should Anyone be Led by you.

David A Garvin – How Google Sold its Engineers on Management

Linda Holbeche and Geoffrey Matthews - Engaged

Alex Gorsky – Johnson and Johnson, CEO

1 FOREWORD

The idea for this dramatic workshop arose following several Conferences and meetings attended during 2013. The workshop was written during the Summer of 2013 and I met with Dr Fida Afiouni from the American University of Beirut in September of that year to ask if we could collaborate on the event involving HR students. At the same time I asked Hywel Simons UK (Welsh) Actor and Director if he would help with the theatrical side of this work and to coach the students in acting skills and direct the workshop. Fortunately, both Dr Fida and Hywel agreed to collaborate.

Why did I feel that this dramatic workshop should be pursued? Well, there seemed to be a sense of frustration from employees of all levels – including Human Resource Professionals – that the workplace was not as happy as it could be. People often commented that employees arrived full of enthusiasm and yet this seemed to have evaporated during the course of the first year of employment if not earlier.

This is a source of immense sadness to the majority of people I meet. The place of work is not meant to be perfect. It cannot be. In most cases it may well be a reflection of the society from where the majority of employees are drawn. This will be the case even though the world we live in now provides the opportunity for employment virtually anywhere in the world. So the workplace cannot be perfect but it can be a place to find meaning, inspiration, learning, development and a sense of achievement.

During the course of my career over many years I have never met anyone who has come to work with the thought in mind "to make a complete mess of things." On the contrary, all of the people I have met have set out wanting to do a great job and learn from the experience.

However, so many times we see this hope dashed and for many people work becomes a place to attend to receive a salary in exchange for a service rendered. Arguably, this arises not only for those who are led by managers but also for the managers themselves. A culture of dissatisfaction can be endemic in the organization and perhaps, for the managers, the palliative may only be the financial reward they receive for carrying out their job.

However, this general air of dissatisfaction is often concealed. Some in the company who are more attuned than others may well detect a whiff of "faint but displeasing odour" in the air but do not have the data to pinpoint from where it is arising. If any manager asks a subordinate "how things are going" the response is often "Yeah, fine". In truth, in most cases that response is likely to mean exactly the opposite and sensing that nothing will change if a direct truth is told, the person dissembles.

Mostly, managers settle for believing the dissembler because it is reassuring to do so and uncomfortable to think otherwise. There is often a yawning gap between the views of the top management team on what their employees think about their work and the ay they are treated and what employees actually believe.

This is why independently run employee engagement surveys are so useful in providing the data that is needed. If Top Managers look at the data with open eyes and accept what is being said to them it is the first step towards creating workplaces which are not perfect but which allow all employees to be heard and to feel fulfilled by the role for which they have been selected and which also they have chosen.

It is true that all the points which are being made here in this foreword and in the dramatic workshop itself could have been made in a traditional presentation or a traditional workshop. However, I am moving away from these as a method to inform and from which learning is derived. Observing audiences as a participant and also as a speaker it is often the case, even with our most talented and gifted speakers, that a point is reached at which the audience is lost. It is only the rare few who have the gift to "hold the audience" throughout the presentation or the workshop. And even with those who have this rare gift there will be "black holes" where the listener will have winked out for some moments. It is rare when one person is speaking for our attention to be held continuously.

As a result the learning we experience can be diminished, can be fleeting. The learning and the understanding is there while we are listening – if we are listening – but as we all know will rapidly fade thereafter. In a matter of days, if not hours, if it as if we had not participated in the event.

I have always been an advocate of development which combines learning with project work and coaching as this reinforces the knowledge which has been provided and transforms it into an endurable and sustainable skill.

The difficulty has often been the attendee retaining the information from the time of delivery. Listening is mostly a poor means of retaining information. Yet when information is provided in dramatic format there seems to be a higher rate of retention. Consider for a moment the ability of all of us to retell the details of a film or theatre drama or the events in a television series. I have watched as colleagues and friends will recount in exact detail the occurrences that have arisen in a drama whether on TV or at the movie theatre. I have watched also as there attention is entirely focused on the action in the drama. They are gripped by the action and the events that are unfolding. Not only is this to do with he desire, as in all stories, to know what happens next. There is more to it than just that.

In a sense the watchers place themselves in the shoes of the participants and maybe feel themselves to be involved in what is going on. You can see it for yourself. If you observe watchers of a programme you will see involuntary body movements and the desire to speak out and at home the characters are often spoken and encouraged or abused depending on the role which they are playing.

In a way we experience the activities vicariously. We feel the things that have happened almost as if they have happened to us. In this sense it is different to hearing from a third party about what has happened to someone else. We do not experience it in the same way. Thus the events become in some way locked into our memories.

Therefore in this dramatic workshop – "Living in the Dark Shadow of Opinion" – we have tried to provide the story of a new employee joining a company or organization. It so happens that the person is joining the Sales Team but the events which arise could occur to any new employee in any Department in any company or organization. Those watching the incidents as they arise will recognize them. Some who watch it may well feel that the workshop is based on their company or organization. But the facts are that the occurrences which arise are typical of mistakes which are made in many organisations. They are not necessarily of themselves serious issues but the cumulative effect is sufficient to take away the spirit and enthusiasm of those who want to belong to the organization. It softly bludgeons the sense of urgency and immediacy necessary to get things done, ruins any chance of innovation so that that although there is movement forward it is painfully slow. CEO's and Boards often wonder why the pace is so slow and why execution of tasks takes so long.

While watching (or reading) the dramatic workshop I am sure that you will identify with many of the events. Some may have happened to you and some you may well have been responsible for whilst leading people. Mostly, we are guilty of carelessness rather than serious intent to make the lives of others difficult. We can change that behaviour with a change in thinking. Alex Gorsky, the CEO of Johnson and Johnson asks this question at interviews: " Tell me about four people whose careers you have made better." Stop to answer that question to yourself right now. If you cannot answer that question quickly enough it is probably because like many of us you are focusing on personal achievement. Yet, if we really are to make changes in the working environment we must focus on the development of others to achieve goals.

Acknowledgements

People

I am indebted to Dr Fida Afiouni, Coordinator of the Masters in HR programme at AUB who has collaborated with me in getting this dramatic workshop from the written word to the state of performance. She has assisted me with a cast drawn from the HR Bachelor and Master Students from the American University of Beirut. The student cast list and those involved in Production are listed below.

My thanks to Hywel Simons, Actor and Director, who gave me sound advice in the dramatic writing of this work

My thanks to all the students of AUB who have taken part in this dramatic workshop from its early beginnings. We rehearsed from September of 2013 through until April of 2014. The final copy of the workshop arises from the many wording changes we made as we practiced over and over again.

In House Production Guide

The idea of producing this dramatic workshop was not only for it to be staged in public places but also for it to be run within companies and organisations. There is no reason why a group of individuals within any company might not use this workshop as an inhouse development activity to improve levels of engagement and commitment. Also in doing so a sense of collaboration and community spirit will be developed because after all "we are all in it together". And by no means least, people will have fun in developing the production. Indeed it can be adapted and amended to suit any organization or company.

To ensure that the workshop happens it will need the following:

- A "Director". It does not necessarily mean a professional theatrical Director but someone who can guide the "actors" in the way the lines should be spoken.
- "Actors". There are five primary roles and two smaller roles. In the script names are left blank for you to include as you wish.
- A stage, auditorium or large room sufficient provide room for the actors to be seen and for upwards of 20-100 people to view.
- Scenery and props. You can be imaginative. Most scenes take place in an office so perhaps a desk, desk items, and a few chairs will be appropriate. Other scenes with employees could be in a rest/lounge area or staff restaurant with appropriate tables and furniture

The production will also need the primary speaker who will comment on what is taking place, provide information and challenge the audience to give opinions and to say how things should be changed for the better. I have left my words in as commentary but they may be changed by the facilitator.

It should not be left at that. The staging of the dramatic workshop inhouse will bring issues to the surface which will require addressing. As soon as possible after the workshop an independent employee engagement survey should be run and group formed from a cross section of staff who will work with experts to analyse the feedback and recommend actions for implementation.

The workshop is just the start. It will pave the way for change and for the creation of a positive environment in which employees at all levels will flourish and achieve not just for themselves but for other employees and stakeholders. Employees will want to do things not just for themselves and to earn a salary but because they genuinely care about the future of the organization and the people who work in it. It will no longer be a case that employees and managers live in "The Dark Shadow of Opinion."

At the conclusion of the dramatic workshop text I have provided a workbook for use by the audience. In Act 3 the HR Manager gives a presentation the facilitator should design a set of slides to be used with that presentation. It will be more effective when run.

Working with Companies

If any company or organization needs help in staging this event as an in house production please contacts us and we will visit you to discuss how we can assist.

If there are any issues other than this which you believe exist in your organization and you would like to bring them to the surface in the form of a dramatic workshop we can also write this for you and help you with the event.

Contact Details

Maurice Collis: maurice.collis@hrworks-me.com or maurice_collis@hotmail.com

Dr Fida Afiouni: fa16@aub.edu.lb

Hywel Simons: hywelsimons@me.com

2 INTRODUCTION

MC: *Welcome everyone. My name is Maurice Collis and for over 35 years I have worked with companies as a Director, Managing Director or Consultant assisting companies with achieving high performance. Most but not all of my Career has been in HR. Speaking at an HR Summit in Beirut not so long ago there was a clear indication from the audience – mostly HR professionals – that it was difficult to be taken seriously.*

There is nothing new in this. It has always been so: joining as a graduate long, long ago and opting for Personnel a colleague who had opted for operations remarked to me in the lift months later "If I was enjoying life in the sun lounge."

Difficult to respond isn't it. As HR professionals we struggle sometimes to demonstrate how and where we add value. Mostly we have accepted the view that like good customer service good HR practice is not noticed. Very bad and exceptional Customer service is noticed and so it is with HR. Regrettably, because mostly we are not ahead of the curve we don't see armies of operators banging on the HR Manager's door to congratulate him or her for outstanding performance. (Pause) But that's what you'd like isn't it.

But the truth is that we as HR professionals have not shown that we are A performers. We have not been stars. From the operators point of view most of the time we distract them from the work that needs doing to generate revenue. They see us a pain in the……. A bit of a nuisance! Irrelevant even. To avoid this and I paraphrase David Ulrich HR needs to pass the "wallet test". And HR passes the wallet test by creating human and organizational capabilities that are better than those of the company's competitors. Simply because the work adds to the bottom line and creates a remarkable work environment. HR actions create value when they create a sustainable competitive advantage. We need to focus on deliverables and not just doables!

So we can change and create value for the company and maybe in future you will see your Manager, Director or C level peers nodding appreciatively at the work that you do.

This dramatic and interactive workshop we are about to show you will help you on this journey. I am assisted in this endeavour by Hywel Simons, who is a professional Actor and Director and who has help me shape this work and Dr Fida Afiouni , Coordinator of the Master in HR programme at the American University of Beirut. We are also indebted to have with us actors who are HR and Masters students and at AUB. My thanks also to AUB who have allowed us to use this magnificent auditorium and to my good friend, Charles Saliba of HRworks and all the team there who have provided so much help to get us where we are.

The workshop we are about to see covers the journey of a new employee to a company. Some of you – maybe many of you – will think that somehow I have tapped in to what happens at your company or organization. Of course, I haven't. The events that we are about to witness are commonplace.

The point is that we do not often penetrate the membrane between what management believes its employees feel about the company and the reality – that is what employees really feel but do not communicate verbally unless to each other.

So we will follow the journey and then debate what we should be doing and how we can measure our success.

One further point. We have provided you with a workbook for you to make comments on the interactions you see. After the first Act is concluded we will ask you to discuss in group and to say what could have been done better. We will collect these and include for the rerun in the Second Act.

Let's begin:

Dramatis Personae

CEO:

HR Manager:

New Employee (Employee 1)

Existing Employee (Employee 2)

Sales Manager

Finance Manager

Operations Manager

Scene 1

Sales Manager : Well, we have concluded our interview and I'm happy to tell you that we are going to offer you a position in Sales. This is a great place to work with really good people and I think you'll fit in well. The HR Department will send you the offer and the details so it's only for me to say that I look forward to working with you.

Employee 1: (shakes hands enthusiastically with Manager) Thank you, Thank You. I promise that I will not let you down.

Light dims on Manager or he freezes. Employee walks away with a huge smile and punches the air, maybe a victory dance.

Employee 1: (*Addressing audience*) I've just been offered a job here. I didn't expect to get the offer so quickly but I am so excited. For sure I am great at Sales and my guess is that they've seen that. The money here is fantastic and the sales commission just great. But it's not that which excites me it's all the other things. Being part of a team, learning from my new boss – that was her back there – and being developed and maybe getting a Sales Manager job myself one day, as long as it's not too far off.

Really, I can't believe it. I have so much to offer and I'm going to do so much here. I'm young. I know I have ability and now I have the opportunity to fly. (*Stops suddenly, remembering*)

My family, I have to tell them. They will be so happy. It's going to make such a difference.

(Exits)

MC: *Most of us have felt that surge of enthusiasm and excitement when a new job is offered. Come on, it's a pretty human reaction. It's like a validation of who we are by someone who does not really know us – and we have probably been selected over other people. We are entitled to feel ….. well special! We've come first in a competition.*

How long does that feeling last? (Looks at audience?)

Why does it fade (Asks Audience)

OK, we hold those thoughts for now. A new HR Manager is joining the Company and is having a conversation with the CEO. Let's look in on the conversation……..

(Cuts to actors)

Scene 2

CEO: Sit down, please sit down. Well, we are so glad you decided to join us.

HR Manager: Thank you, I'm really looking forward to the challenges ahead. I'm a great believer in unlocking the potential of people as you know. We talked about it at my interview.

CEO: Yes, yes, I know. We pay well here – top dollar as you know from your offer - and we look for people who can hit the ground running. Like you, I knew as soon as I clapped eyes on you that you were the right one for us. Good in hiring, payroll, personnel procedures and all the Labour Law issues. Just what we need.

HR Manager: Yes, I can deal with all of the Personnel administration issues it's true.......

CEO: I know, I know and we are very happy that you are here.

CEO Freezes

HR Manager: (turns to audience) I hear an alarm bell already. That is disappointing. Oh, I do hope we will be able to be more than just be administrators. I have some superb ideas that I would like to introduce. Did I miss something at the interview. Interview? Well that's a thought too. It was just one interview, wasn't it?

CEO Unfreezes

CEO: So, you have any questions for me at the moment. Anything I can do to help you settle in more easily.

HR Manager: Well now I'm here it would be very useful to see the Business Plan so that I can align the HR strategy with your vision so that we improve capability.

CEO: *(Opens mouth and looks confused)* Business Plan? You want to look at it? OK, well we'll come to that in good time. You settle in first and get the basics .....aligned ...and then we'll *(Slowly)* come to the business Plan. Anything else?

HR Manager: How committed and motivated do you think the employees are?

CEO: *(Emphatically)* Very! Very!

HR Manager: How do you know, if I may ask?

CEO: Well I just know. I walk the job...... you know, I walk the job. *(Then hurriedly)* Good! Well, let's meet again soon and we can discuss how you're getting on. Right! Good with you?

HR Manager: (Enthusiasm dropping) Yes, let's meet again. Thank you.

HR Manager rises from seat and exits. CEO drums fingers on desk, makes a face as if is considering what the HR Manager has said and then shrugs it all off.

Switch to MC

MC: Hmmm! The HR Manager doesn't seem too happy now. I wonder why that is. Has he/she been blinded by the dollar sign. Obviously, a good person but maybe the CEO needs some education. What are your thoughts at the moment.

(Feedback from audience)

MC: *Thank You. Let's now have a look at how the enthusiastic new employee is getting on.*

Scene 3

New Employee 1: Thanks for helping me these last weeks. You've been great.

Employee 2 : No problem! I like to help new ones coming in. Some make it and some don't. How are you finding it?

New Employee 1: (Cautious) O.......K, I guess. I was hoping for a longer and more informative induction, you know to get to know the way of doing things. *(Brightly)* But overall the company is good and we have a good reputation out there. I think it will change and I think you know I can help with the change.

Employee 2: Good luck with trying to change things, (*Name*). Looks to me like you've been thrown in at the deep end, huh? I know at the interview they said you would have this and that during your induction and you would get training etc etc. Right?

New Employee 1 : Yes, how do you know that?

Employee 2 : Been there, done that, got the T shirt. We all go through the public relations and marketing bull when we join. Don't worry, though I'll give you all the help I can. I keep running out of Sales partners so I want you to do well. You know like you said this company is well meaning and the products are good and the service we deliver is pretty good and we get paid really well. But that's as far as it goes. *(Pause)* By the way, what does the boss say to you about how you're doing? You are coming to the end of your probation period, aren't you?

New Employee 1: *(Frowns)* Yes I am. You know I was expecting to agree targets and objectives and have frequent reviews during my probation. But none of this happened. I was given a territory as you know and I've got on with it. To be honest you've helped me more than the Boss. My meetings with her don't touch performance. They get close to it but it seems to drift away from it.

Employee 2: How do you mean? (*Freezes*)

New Employee moves to new seat where Boss is present

New Employee 1: I've come for our meeting

Sales Manager: *(Distracted)* Yes, come in and sit down. (*Does not look at employee and is completing a text or reading papers*). Ok, how are things going?

New Employee 1: *(Hesitant)* OK, I think bearing in mind that I'm new to this product. I'm learning fast.

Sales Manager: Your predecessor was faster. The figures were better.

New Employee 1: Yes, I meant to ask you about that. I know you said you'd agree targets when I completed probation but I'd like some things to aim at.

Sales Manager: We will come to it. Your performance is not bad but it could be better. Just go out there and try harder.

New Employee 1: Try harder? Can you give me some advice, guidance.

Sales Manager: You've been in Sales a while. You don't need it. Just do what you did before. I'm sure it'll be fine. OK so get on with it. We'll meet next week.

New Employee 1: But……. *(Changes mind and starts to leave)*

Sales Manager: Oh Yeah and be careful when you're visiting XYZ company. They complained about you. Said you arrived late.

New Employee 1 : But…..

Sales Manager: Just get on with it.

New Employee leaves and rejoins Employee who unfreezes

Employee 2: *(laughs)* Oh, yes that's our Boss. Look I'll come with you on a visit and see what you're doing and give some tips if you want.

New Employee 1: *(Enthusiastic)* Yes, if you can spare the time. That would be great. Thanks.

Employee 2: And don't worry about XYZ. They always say we're late. I bet you were waiting in the lobby. They do it so they can squeeze us on price.

New Employee 1: *(In surprise)* How did you know….. *(voice trails away)*

Employee 2 smiles knowingly at the other. Scene fades.

MC Intervention

MC: Does this sound familiar. Ok we are using Sales as this is an easy area in which to provide examples but you will surely find it in other functions as well. The truth is we rarely equip our managers to assist with effective orientation and onboarding. This is an opportunity to maintain that enthusiasm we saw on the face of our new employee when he/she got the news. They arrive, we breathe a sigh of relief and let them get on with it. And also we do not teach our Managers the art of Performance Management. We assume they can do it.

And when people are not trained effectively and there are no measures or targets the dark shadow of opinion flourishes.

But before we come to that: The Employee. He/she is a jewel isn't he/she. The question is do the senior management team know it? Remember this both employees are probably thinking "I don't care how much you know until I know how much you care."

Now let's look at the dark work of opinion?

Scene 4

CEO: I've asked you to join us as Sales Manager is not happy with (*Employee 1 Name*).

CEO returns to ask papers

HR Manager: *(addressing Sales Manager)* Ok, what do the probation reports say?

Sales Manager: Behind targets. I expected better based on what had been done before.

HR Manager: Behind by how much, if I may ask? Also what did you say at the review meetings.

Sales Manager: About 10% behind the target.

HR Manager: What did *(Employee 1 name)* say at the review meetings?

Sales Manager: He/She said she would try harder and I gave every possible encouragement to do so.

HR Manager: I don't think you've really talked this through at review meetings, have you. I know it's not easy.

Sales Manager: Well….. You know I thought *(Employee 1 name)* would be as good as the last one.

HR Manager: That person was here for 3 years. Are the sales progressing every month?

Sales Manager: Yes I think so but I'm not really sure if he/she is one of us, you know

HR Manager: What makes you say that?

Sales Manager: Well……

HR Manager: The three month probation is completed tomorrow. If you're thinking of a termination you've left it too late under probation rules.

Sales Manager: Well…….I'll have to struggle with him/her then I guess. The CEO knows we have tough targets so…….

CEO: You are the Manager of your Department *(Sales Manager name)*, so manage please. Overall you're not that far away and I expect you to get your targets on track including the ones for the new person. What's the name again?

Sales Manager: *(Employee 1 Name)*

Freeze

MC Intervention

MC: (*To HR Manager who unfreezes) Well, what about you. Did you have targets during probation and an effective onboarding? Did the CEO meet you every month to review?*

HR Manager: I prepared the targets myself but to be honest I weighted them heavily in personnel administration targets and I organized my own on boarding effectively. I set up the meetings with the CEO and we went through – but to be frank it was onesided and totally non-motivational.

(HR Manager looks at MC's expression)

I'm working on it!!

HR Manager freezes

MC: *(Addresses Audience)* What can we learn from the exchange between the HR Manager and the Sales Manager? What other areas of concern did you notice?

MC co-ordinates discussion

MC: OK let's go back to this group and see what happens next......

Group Unfreeze

Scene 5

CEO: Thanks Sales Manager. Do your best to get *(Employee 1 name)* up to speed. The HR Manager will help you, I'm sure. Well, I need to talk to *(HR Manager name)* about something so......

Sales Manager leaves

CEO: (Glances at door) Have you seen the Sales figures for this month. They are flat and customer complaints are up with Operations blaming Sales and vice versa. I am seeing the Finance Manager after you as Receivables are rising and general expenses increasing. If it goes on for too long it will hit cash flow and then nobody will be happy if payroll is delayed.

CEO stays silent, pauses, looks at papers and tosses them aside

CEO: *(mumbles almost to self)* The people are useless. (*Then louder)* You know I think the people are useless. We'd be better off if we got rid of most and started again. *(pause)* We have to get better hires.

(Points finger at HR Manager) You, You are going to have to do better.

HR Manager: *(Places finger at chest and mouths)* Me? *(Pauses)* They are useless based on what?

CEO: Based on our performance. Look at it. *Points at figures.*

HR Manager: Are you sure it's the employees? Maybe we are doing something wrong?

CEO: *(Snorts in derision)* Pffffff!! We pay them very well and they are not performing as they should. That's it. And you know what, the acquisition we are making will bring in better people and that will show them how it's done.

HR Manager: *(In surprise)* Acquisition? What acquisition?

Freeze

CEO awakes and looks at MC

MC: *(to CEO)* You didn't tell her about the acquisition? Anyone in fact did you?

CEO: It was commercially confidential. I needed to keep it secret – for a while at least anyway

MC: *(Doubtfully)* O.....K! Always a good get out that one. (Pause) Are you happy with the way things are going? Do you feel in control?

CEO: *(Hesitantly)* Of course I.....Of Course I do. We've just go to do.....some......take some direct action to improve things. That's......that's all.

MC: That sounds very interesting to me.

CEO gives MC an inquiring look and freezes

MC: *(To audience)* What further picture is emerging?

After co-ordinating discussion

Let's now see if the Employees have comments on the way they are led.

Scene 6

Employee 2: So how are you getting on with changing things around here. Any luck?

New Employee 1: *Shrugs.* No, not much luck with that I am sorry to say.

Employee 2: By the way, do you sense that something is not right? The Managers look like they are going crazy and soon they'll be blaming us for poor performance. You watch out. I've heard it being said that we don't work hard enough.

New Employee 1: That's not fair. We do.

Employee 2: Of course we do but it doesn't matter. They don't listen to us and don't tell us anything. It's all one way, my friend.

New Employee 1: But deep down they are all good people. There must be a way to get a change.

Employee 2: Haven't you worked it out yet. There is no professional recruitment here, no real orientation or onboarding, no worthwhile training, no people friendly HR policies, no recognition, no praise, no communication and to top it all no trust.

New Employee 1: *(Considering what was said)* If all that is true then why do you stay. You've been here quite a while.

Employee 2: *(Laughs and wags finger at employee)* Just like you my friend: I'm a hopeless optimist.

They both laugh

Employee 2: *(Continues)* Incidentally, have you heard about the acquisition

New Employee 1: *(In surprise)* No, I haven't.

Employee: *(With a wry smile)* See what I mean. *(Hold hands together as if in prayer and looks upward)* It will change. It will change.

Scene Freezes

MC: *Addresses the audience.* What is happening? Is it common? Do you think it might be happening in your companies and organisations.

Organises questions and continues

Let's go back now and see how the CEO and HR Manager are dealing with things:

Cut to CEO and HR Manager

Scene 7

CEO: We'll have the new appraisal form used from this quarter. You know the one that was launched just before you arrived. People will be using it now. This should help us get back on track I think. Don't you?

HR Manager: *(Frowns)* Talking to people it seems the form has been changed a number of times. In fact every time a new HR Manager arrives. *(CEO's face looks horrified).* Don't worry I won't change it. But I'll let you into a secret. It will be useless. Performance Management is not about the form; it's about developing people to manage performance.

CEO: Well, we'll see. By the way we're introducing a new swipe card system for everyone. *(Hurriedly)* We agreed this before you arrived. It means that people will swipe their card when they come in and when they leave. Installation starts tomorrow

HR Manager looks amazed

HR Manager: We haven't communicated this to employees and explained the reason.

CEO: We don't have to do we. It's Health and Safety. You know we'll be aware of who is here in case there is a fire. Stuff like that.

HR Manager: You know that if you don't communicate a message the employees will put their own view on it. They'll say you don't trust them.

CEO: *(sounding false)* No, of course not. We do, we do.

HR Manager: It's like the acquisition. Same thing.

CEO: *(getting angry)* Are you serious. Do they need to know the ins and outs of everything? Everything?

Freezes and cuts to MC

MC: (To audience) Let me show you something. I need a drawing of a house please

Asks all the attendees to draw a house. As simple or as ornate as they like. If anyone asks questions like what sort of house it is ignored or given the instruction to be creative. When they have completed the exercise MC asks the attendees to hold up their drawings. He goes around the room saying "No that's not what I wanted" and then provides the explanation. Most Managers ask for something to be done and assume the subordinate understands. If the subordinate and the manager do not clarify for understanding the "wrong house" will result.

MC Continues

MC: *The management of performance is not easy. Most people give a general outline as we saw with the house example and then complain that they have not got what they wanted. It requires care and communication for understanding on both sides. But typically it's a case of "you know what to do, just get on with it."*

Now let's see a section of the review between the Sales Manager and the new employee

Cuts to meeting

Scene 8

Sales Manager: Well as you know you got through your probation. *(clears throat)* These are the targets and how you did against them. *(Passes a paper to the Employee)*

You can do better, I know.

Employee 1: Why didn't you show me the targets when I joined?

Sales Manager: Well it was probation, you know, and so this is what you can do for the coming quarter. You can do it?

Employee 1: Well now I know what I'm aiming at yes, I think I can.

Sales Manager: I'll send you on a course also. It will help. OK, Good luck then.

Employee 1: Before I go. I'd like to ask you about the acquisition I've heard about and my future as far as development and promotion is concerned. It may be a bit early but I'm interested in the plan.

Sales Manager: *(blusters) (Mumbles)* Acquisition? *(Pauses)* Uh!......We can talk about that again. I have someone coming in so………

Employee 1: *(Leaving and mutters)* Hah! He/She doesn't know anything about this acquisition. It's obvious.

Some weeks have passed by

MC: Two months have passed so let's now look in on the conversation between the two Employees.

Cuts to conversation with employees.

Scene 9

Employee 2: So all going well? So how did that training go?

New Employee 1: I don't know. Not so good, I suppose. Of course as I am getting more used to the market my sales are getting better but it's never good enough. My good work is overlooked and we focus on where we didn't get the business. If I ask for specifics he/she just gets irritated and tells me to get out and ..

Both Together: …..Just do it *(They laugh)*

Employee 2: And the course ?

New Employee 1: It was a waste of time. It was basic selling. I'd been on it before.

Employee 2: (*Laughs*) I said you'd never change it. There's no dialogue here and no seeing the employee point of view. You know you can hear them say here "People are our most important resource". It's rubbish, expendable resource more like. All one way. (*Pauses*) Hey did I tell you about my son.

New Employee 1: I heard about it but tell me more.

Employee 2: Well this is what happened. He needed to go into hospital for a while and I wanted to change my hours so I could visit. They wouldn't do it. (*Mimics an official voice*) "9am until 5.30pm are the hours without exception". They told me I could take it as unpaid leave.. That's what they told me. I was willing to work evenings and weekends and more to make it up – but nothing.

New Employee 1: Did you go see that new HR Manager. I think he'd be reasonable.

Employee 2: He/she is trying but he has a lot of culture to change. (*Pauses*) Anyway, I have to tell you something: they have knocked all of the optimism out of me, sooooo........I'm leaving.

New Employee 1: What???

Employee 2: Come on, you must have seen the signs. I've been thinking about it for a while. I get a lot of offers as it happens. But...but this last incident with my son did it for me. It's a good offer...not a lot more than I'm getting here but after I while with development I get to manage a team.

New Employee 1: (*dismayed*) But you are the best we have in Sales, the best. (*Lost in thought*) How can I survive here if you're not around ?

Employee 2: The best? They obviously don't think so. Did you hear about XYZ getting promoted? How did that happen? And you know it wasn't even advertised. Pffff!!

Both are lost in thought as the CEO enters.

CEO: Aha! Thinking of new ideas for us, that's great. This is exactly the thing we need. You see I always say that our employees are our best resource.

(if audience laughs or applauds the CEO turns to the audience in perplexity)

 CEO: So how are things? How are you doing? We are picking up you know? Revenues are better.

Employees: *(Both speak together but words say one thing and body language another)* Yes all is fine, thank you. It's good. Enjoying the work. Good to see you.

CEO: Excellent, well keep up the good work. We can't do it without you.

(Walks away with self satisfied smile)

Freeze and cut to MC:

MC: (Addresses Audience) *When we hear anyone say "People are our most important asset" it is a platitude. It means nothing. The only way it can be so is if we invest time and resources in helping employees at all levels to* *become competent and committed.*

I wonder what you are thinking about our CEO. We will discuss more on this later. In a recent article by David A Garvin in the December 2013 edition of HBR. He comments on the research undertaken at Google where they identified 8 key behaviours by the most effective managers. They are:

(i) Good coach (ii) Empowers the team and does not micromanage (iii) Expresses interest in and concern for team members success and personal well being (iv) Is productive and results oriented (v) Is a good communicator – listens and shares information (vi) Helps with Career Development (vii) Has a clear vision and strategy for the team (viii) Has key technical skills that help him or her advise the team.

Makes you wonder about the managers at this company I think?

MC organizes discussion

MC: *Continues*

The new employee's enthusiasm through a series of setbacks has completely disappeared. He/she will still turn up for work as he/she needs the money but will have become actively disengaged. This process of disengaging does not happen overnight. There is an established sequence of events. There is a high probability that some of you in this room are on this journey right now. The sequence is as follows:

- *Starts new job with enthusiasm*
- *Questions the decision to accept the job*
- *Thinks seriously about quitting*
- *Tries to change things*
- *Resolves to quit*
- *Considers the cost of quitting*
- *Passively seeks another job, brushes up CV*
- *Prepares actively to seek*
- *Actively seeks*
- *Gets new job offer*
- *Quits to accept new job or quits with out a job or stays and disengages*

This decision to disengage is normally triggered by one single event. This is normally one of the following:

- *Discovering you are underpaid compared to peers doing the same job*
- *Realising that you are not in line for promotion*
- *Pressured to make unreasonable personal or family sacrifices*
- *Being asked to perform menial duties*
- *Petty and unreasonable enforcement of authority*
- *Denied request for family leave*
- *A close colleague quitting or terminated*
- *Disagreement with a boss*
- *Conflict with a co-worker*
- *Unexpectedly low performance rating*
- *Low pay increase or no pay increase*

- *Passed over for promotion*
- *Realising the job is different to that promised*
- *Being transferred*
- *Replacement of hiring boss with a new boss*
- *Being asked to do something unethical*
- *Racial or sexual harassment*

You are able to detect when this has arisen. Individuals who have been triggered into disengagement display the following:

- *Avoid eye contact*
- *Stop smiling or greeting*
- *Give less energy and effort*
- *Arrive later*
- *Leave earlier*
- *Have burst of anger or frustration*
- *Participate less at meetings*
- *Exhibit passive noncompliance*
- *Exhibit active resistance*
- *Absent more often*
- *Miss Deadlines*
- *Increase community involvement and networking*

When people have disengaged these are the behaviours they show. Some refer to it as "presenteeism". They are at work but not active. In the army they refer to them as ROAD warriors – 'retired on active duty'.

What we need to remember is this: the essence of engagement is trust, fairness and delivery on promises. If these are not present you can be sure that as trust goes down so does speed of execution and costs will inevitably go up.

Let's now go back to a conversation between the CEO, the HR Manager, Sales Manager, Ops Manager and Finance Manager

Scene 10

CEO: There's a little improvement but you know I think we need to kick start things a little. There is an air of complacency. Maybe we should let a few go to shake up the others!!.

Ops Manager: I'd be in favour of that. We need to shake things up. What do you think (Sales Manager). Some of your people could do with a shock.

Sales Manager: Umm, yes we could do something I think. You maybe right.

CEO: What do you think (*Finance Manager name*) ?

Finance Manager: (*Playing with calculator*) I'm always up to reduce cost. Can we hire cheaper. Let's do it

HR Manager: Wait, wait, wait, Based on what?

CEO: Well performance of course.

HR Manager *(sighs and pauses)* You should now also that *(Employee 2)* has resigned.

CEO: What! I saw *(Employee 2)* the other day and he/she seemed fine. Lost in thought thinking up ideas. What happened *(Sales Manager name)?*.

Sales Manager: Ran out of steam, I think. You know Sales guys. They get tired of the product and want to move on to something new.

CEO: *(Unsure)* Hmmm!

HR Manager: Are you sure that's the real reason *(Sales Manager name)*? And you know that *(Employee 1 name)* is thinking of leaving also. He/she came to see me.

CEO: *(mumbles)* No loss there.

Sales Manager: Yes, Yes. You are right of course.

Ops Manager: Just as well we keep things on the road you know. Sales guys! Huh!!

HR Manager: *(Hesitantly)* But look, what if the performance problem is us? What if it is things we are doing and not doing?

CEO: *(Shrugs)* Ridiculous! How can it be! We are just getting the wrong people.

Sales Manager , Finance Manager and Ops Manager: (Laugh at the suggestion)

CEO: (*Open mouthed)*

HR Manager: *(makes as if to speak but stops and frowns)*

Scene freezes. HR Manager stands and looks at audience and MC.

HR Manager: You know I have no answers because I have no evidence. I just have my feelings. My intuition. But I can't back it up, can I??

Freeze and cut to MC

MC: I'm sure that many people here recognize some of these issues although we recognize that many of the scenes are caricatures. Nevertheless there is truth here in what takes place. Often we know what the situation is but there is a huge chasm between "knowing" and doing".

Conventional wisdom and Marcus Buckingham along with many other gurus tell us that the art of being a Great Leader lies in:

- *Select a Person*
- *Set expectations*
- *Motivate*
- *Develop*

Simple really isn't it but rarely do we do all four.

So as businesses we need to understand our Employee Value Proposition. This is effectively the WIIFM factor potential employees. WIIFM – that's what's in it for me. The progress of an individual in a company is based on the following and follows Maslow's Hierarchy of Needs theory:

- *I want a job*
- *I want fair pay*

- *I want the benefits I want (explain the enlarged I)*
- *I want to learn more to grow in my career*
- *I want to feel like I belong here*
- *I LOVE WORKING FOR YOU*

For companies and organisations it's all about building a cadre of employees who are RAVING FANS.

To ensure that employees become raving fans we need to have a Total Reward Strategy. I'm sure most of you are aware of this and as you know Marcus Buckingham argues that it focuses on the following five elements:

- *Pay*
- *Benefits*
- *Work-Life*
- *Performance & Recognition*
- *Development & Career Opportunities*

David Ulrich takes it a little further. He states that the EVP is:

- *Vision: the company has a clear sense of the future that engages heart and minds*
- *Opportunity: Work provides the chance to grow personally and professionally*
- *Incentive: Fair and equitable package*
- *Impact: The work makes a difference or creates meaning*
- *Community: The social environment includes being part of a team and working with others who care about what they do.*
- *Communication: The flow of information is two way, so employees are informed about what is going on.*
- *Experimentation: Working hours, dress and other policies are flexible and designed to adapt to the needs of both the company and employee.*

There are other facts we need to understand also:

It used to be said that structure follows strategy but that is now old thinking. Now it is likely that capabilities follow strategy.

The work of Mark Huselid, Brina Becker and Richard Beatty has shown that companies who excel in the following capabilities:

- *Speed*
- *Talent*
- *Learning*
- *Shared Mindset*
- *Innovation*
- *Accountability*

Significantly outperformed lower capability companies in productivity, profitability and shareholder value.

So in the context of improving what we have seen in this dramatic representation in groups I would like you to consider what policies and practices you would have in place. If these policies were in place and working how would it ensure that performance is improved and disintegration avoided.

Once you have done this you will work with the actors to reshape the scenes based on your revised Employee Value Proposition.

We have already prepared a script for how a great company would organize this but there are many certainties in life and one of them is that someone will always come up with an idea or more which should be included.

How does that sound. Everybody clear on what is required?

Intermission

Attendees work on EVP in groups and with involvement from actors. They will be given a copy of the script from Act I to refresh their memories on the bad things which occurred.

They will also fashion their own ideas of how each scene should be run and what practices and policies would ensure that in fact these employees are "Raving Fans.

4 ACT TWO

MC: *Ok, in the first part of this dramatic workshop we saw how even when you are well meaning things can go wrong. You have had a chance to work with us to provide input as to how the company could do better. Let's go back and remind ourselves of the young person who was selected for the position in Sales. Based on what we think and your input you will see some significant variations.*

Here they are and the Sales Manager is just about to speak:

Scene 1

Sales Manager: Well, we have concluded our selection process and I'm happy to tell you that we are going to you a position in Sales. You did well in your interviews with other Managers as well as with me and we feel that you have the right behavioural fit for the company. The Sales team were impressed with you. I'll share with you the test results later as I'm sure at the moment you want to let your family know about the offer. I want you to know and I hope you've felt that this is a great place to work with really good people and we think you'll fit in well. I am going to arrange for *(Employee 2 name)* to be your "buddy" during the onboarding process. He/she will guide you through and be able to answer any immediate questions you need answers to. That doesn't mean you won't be meeting me regularly as we will have structured meetings to see how your getting along and how we enable the transition so you are completely successful during the probation period. Anyway, that's enough from me. The HR Department will send you the offer and the details so it's only for me now to say that I look forward to working with you. Anything you'd like to ask me now before you leave?

Employee 1: (shakes hands enthusiastically with Manager) Thank you, Thank You. I promise that I will not let you down. I'm sure I have a thousand questions but right now I can't think of one.

Sales Manager: *(laughing)* Don't worry we can go through them when you are ready. Call back to see me at any time.

Light dims on Manager or he freezes. Employee walks away with a huge smile and punches the air, maybe a victory dance.

Employee 1: *(Addressing audience)* I've just been offered a job here. The selection process was so detailed – test and interviews with so many. They took so much care that I thought they'd never offer me a job but now I am so excited. To get through that selection process! Wow! For sure I am great at Sales and my guess is that they've seen that. The money here is fantastic and the sales commission just great. But it's not that which excites me it's all the other things. Being part of a team, learning from my new boss – that was her back there – and being developed and maybe getting a Sales Manager job myself one day, as long as it's not too far off.

Really, I can't believe it. I have so much to offer and I'm going to do so much here. I'm young. I know I have ability and now I have the opportunity to fly. (*Stops suddenly, remembering)*

My family, I have to tell them. They will be so happy. It's going to make such a difference.

(Exits and cut to MC)

MC: *There is a subtle change here isn't there? What has happened here that was different from before? That feeling of excitement is there but what is different this time?*

(Takes questions and ideas from audience)

OK, now if you remember last time the HR Manager was also joining at around the same time. Now let's catch up with the differences we see here in the conversation with the CEO.

(Cuts to Actors)

Scene 2

CEO: Sit down, please sit down. Well, we are so glad you decided to join us. You came through quite an arduous selection process.

HR Manager: Thank you, I'm very happy it was thorough. I like that approach and actually it gives us both the opportunity to decide if we are right for each other.

CEO: I agree. We'd rather not hire than take on somebody who is unlikely to make it through the onboarding process. You know better than me that it's not the candidate's fault if that happens. It means we failed in our job and the consequences for an employee can be disastrous.

HR Manager: You know I wish all companies looked at it that way and that is what is refreshing about this company. So, I'm really looking forward to the challenges ahead. I'm a great believer in unlocking the potential of people as you know. We talked about it at my interview.

CEO: Yes, yes, I know. We pay well here – top dollar as you know from your offer - but we know also that people are looking for people development and the opportunity to show how they can perform. We selected you for that ability and more. Payroll, personnel procedures and so are one thing but we need you to help us devise a way to be better at true HR and to provide us with measures.

HR Manager: Thanks, I am really looking forward to it

CEO: I know, and we are very happy that you are here. I would like us to meet weekly and discuss how you are getting on. We'll set some goals for your first three months. We'll involve some of your team and other people in it as well so that it's collective. We've seen that it's important that your own team sees you as adding value and that your peer groups do as well. Everyone breathes a sigh of relief then that we've made the right hiring decision. How does that sound to you?

HR Manager: *(Enthusiastically)* Great! I like the idea.

CEO Freezes

HR Manager: (turns to audience) I can't believe this. I thought it might be a case of "sink or swim". We all know what normally happens. Someone is hired, everyone breathes a sigh of relief and just wants the new person to get on with it. This attitude is quite amazing.

CEO Unfreezes

CEO: So, you have any questions for me at the moment. Anything I can do to help you settle in more easily.

HR Manager: Well now I'm here it would be very useful to see the Business Plan so that I can align the HR strategy with your vision so that we improve capability.

CEO: *(Smiles)* I was waiting for you to ask. *(Gives HR Manager a copy)* We've lived and breathed this to the point where we can't see the wood for the trees. So a fresh eye looking at it is going to be very good for us. Any other questions?

HR Manager: How committed and motivated do you think the employees are?

CEO: *(Thoughtfully)* That's a good question. I'm tempted to say "very" but the truth is we don't know. We sense that all is OK but we need your guidance here.

HR Manager: Why are you tempted to say "very" if you don't mind my asking

CEO: Well I guess from the body language . I walk the job, you see. And all the management team talk to people and seek feedback but there is always a nagging feeling that they might just be saying it because we are who we are. Give it some thought and come up with a plan. We can look at it then. It's a possible project to deal with during your onboarding.

HR Manager: (Enthusiastically) Nice idea. Thank you.

HR Manager rises from seat and exits. CEO drums fingers on desk and is nodding with contentment.

Switch to MC

MC: *What things did we hear in this exchange. In Act 1 we sensed that the HR Manager had doubts. Why are there no doubts this time? What issues are being addressed?*

(Feedback from audience)

MC: *Ok while all this has been going on of course the employee we met at the beginning has commenced work. Now let's see how she is getting on this time.*

Scene 3

New Employee 1: Thanks for helping me these last weeks. You've been great. The really good thing about it is that the questions I feel awkward about asking the boss is easier when I ask you. And you've given me the insight on each person we deal with and how to behave with them. It's helped me so much.

Employee 2 : No problem! I like to help new ones coming in and so I was delighted when HR and our boss asked me to take on this role also. Since we started this "buddy" system quite a while back we rarely lose anyone now?

New Employee 1: *(Brightly)* I'm not surprised. Overall the company is good and we have a good reputation out there with our service, I know. Nothing is ever perfect though but this company accepts that you aren't and helps you. I've never experienced it before.

Employee 2: Good! Now the boss agreed objectives with you so could get moving on things. How is that going?

New Employee 1: Really good. I was expecting just to be given a territory but the boss has been really helpful

Employee 2: He/She's not the best communicator and knows that and is working on that. But he/she will do her best to get you up to speed.

New Employee 1: *(Smiling)* I know. He/She was quite patient with reasonable objectives to be honest. He/She could have killed me but didn't. I came out from a meeting with her/him this afternoon.

Employee 2 : Tell me how it went? *(Freezes)*

New Employee moves to new seat where Boss is present

New Employee 1: Good afternoon. Good to see you. I've come for our 4pm meeting

Sales Manager: *(Gets focussed)* Yes, come in and sit down. *(Gives full attention to employee)*. Ok, how are things going? It's been exactly a month now since you joined.

New Employee 1: *(Hesitant)* OK, I think bearing in mind that I'm new to this product. I'm learning fast.

Sales Manager: Yes you are. I'm pleased with your integration to be honest. Now remind me what we agreed you would do in your first month.

New Employee: Well there were four. You asked me to (i) Visit all my current client list to introduce myself (ii) acquire full product knowledge (iii) visit and meet the operations team and lastly to acquire two new clients and obtain $8,000 of new business from existing clients.

Sales Manager: OK and how do you think your performance rates.

New Employee: I'm a bit disappointed to be honest. I thought I could have done better.

Sales Manager: *(producing a paper)* Well let's go through it. (i) Client list – achieved and I had some good feedback regarding you from many of the clients. (ii) Product knowledge. Ok I tested you last Friday if you recollect and you achieved around 90%. That's pretty good for first month. (iii) You've visited the operations team and accredited yourself well (iv) You picked up one new client and $6,000 in business from existing clients.

I set you a tough set of activities for month 1 to stretch you and you've made solid progress. And when it comes to the new client you've brought in well that's $10k a month and we've been trying to get them for the last two years.

New Employee 1: *(with self deprecation)* It was easy. I've known them for a long time.

Sales Manager: Easy for you maybe but not for the rest of us. Big well done. I'm really pleased with your progress. And tell me about your collaboration with *(Employee 2 name)*? How is that developing?

New Employee 1: It's a great idea to do that. I've learned a lot and will continue to do so. Thank you for pairing me with her/him.

Sales Manager: *(with a smile)* And what did you learn from the complaint about you from XYZ company?

Employee: *(Surprised)* I was worried at first but when *(Employee 2 name)* told me that they complain to try and get free services well I understood a lot more. Terrible thing to do though!

Sales Manager: I'm speaking with their Director about this so we will resolve it. Anyway, I just want to say congratulations now on the way you are progressing. Let's meet at 2pm tomorrow and if you can come with some suggested new targets we'll go through and agree. Ok with you.

Employee 1: *(Smiling)* Yes, thank you.

New Employee leaves and rejoins Employee who unfreezes

Employee 2: *(laughs)* Well that was pretty good. The boss is getting expert and just as well I tipped you off on XYX. I think you would have had nightmares. Look if you like I'll have a look at your suggested targets before you go in and give some thoughts.

New Employee 1: *(Enthusiastic)* Yes, if you can spare the time. That would be great. Thanks.

Scene fades.

MC Intervention

MC: *What is different about this meeting? Is the Sales Manager too soft do you think? Would another employee really help like this?*

MC organizes questions

MC: *Ok, now let's look in on another meeting. We have the CEO, HR Manager and Sales Manager and they are about to talk about the new employee if you recollect*

Scene 4

CEO: I've asked you to join us as the Sales Manager wants to review the probation and Onboarding of *(New Employee name)*.

CEO hands discussion to the Sales Manager and remains alert

HR Manager: *(addressing Sales Manager)* I've read your reports. They are very good.

Sales Manager: He/She is slightly behind sales targets but has managed to get a contract that we've not been able to manage before. He/She is good with the team and peers and there is great feedback from the clients.

CEO: *(with a smile)* Even XYZ, I hear. They are saying nice things also.

Sales Manager: They are still trying the same old complaint tricks to see if a discount is possible but *(Employee 2 name)* tipped him/her off on how they play the game. I'm dealing with the problem at XYZ.

CEO: I'll speak to the MD also. It's time they dropped this game. *(Turns to HR Manager)* It is something that happens from time to time but thankfully not often. A client continuously complains to get a discount or a freebie.

HR Manager: *Nods in understanding* So no major problem here for us.

Sales Manager: No, no problem but an observation for our future hires

HR Manager: Go on

Sales Manager: Well, we always hire people who know how to sell that's for sure and we can divide them into two types, I think – those who are achievement oriented and those who have empathy. Funny thing is that those who have the empathy as a prime driver seem to get more sales. The aggressive go getters still get good sales of course but the really big stuff, I think, comes from those with empathy. I just wondered if we could check the tests and psychometric data

HR Manager: Yes that's a really good idea. *(thinking)* You've given me some other things to think about also. Let me work on it.

Sales Manager: Great.

CEO: *(addressing HR manager)* You know, we've always felt that the things we do are really good but we've never been able to quantify it. I'd like you to address that.

HR Manager: Music to my ears. Let me work on a presentation for the team.

CEO: *(Addressing Sales Manager)* Nice call on that *(Sales Manager name)*. I think you're on to something here. Well done. We'll see you later. *(CEO rises indicating it's time for Sales Manager to leave)*

Sales Manager: *(Smiles broadly)* Thanks. Bye

CEO: You wouldn't have recognized *(Sales Manager name)* a couple of years ago. He/She was focused on the task but was not team or individual oriented. From a personality point of view he/she probably still is task oriented.

HR Manager: You made the objectives and targets more people oriented, didn't you.

CEO: *(Smiles)* It worked and you know I firmly believe you get more of the behaviour you reward. There 's no point in my beating her/him or anyone else for the things they will never be good at.

Freeze

MC Intervention

MC: (*To HR Manager who unfreezes)* So what are you thinking now? Do you think you've come to the right place?

HR Manager: It's refreshing! We are thinking about what we can do to enable things to happen rather than hoping for the best but I have my part to do also. It's true that this is a good place to work but now we need to quantify it and keep judging ourselves against the measures.

MC: What do you think will happen when you've defined the measures that indicate the worth of employees – and by default HR who are ultimately responsible for people matters?

HR Manager: I ……. *(MC waves hand and HR Manager freezes)*

HR Manager freezes

MC: (*Addresses Audience*) (*Shrugs*) *Well Actually I know what he/she is going to say. But let me ask you. Firstly, what can we learn from the exchange between the HR manager and the Sales Manager which also involved the CEO? Secondly what is going to happen when people measures are in place?*

MC co-ordinates discussion

MC: *OK lets go back to this group and see what happens next……*

Group Unfreeze

Scene 5

CEO: (*Enthusiastically*) Incidentally, Have you seen the Sales figures for this month. They are on the way up and customer satisfaction is on the rise. You know, in my view, it's not just increased sales it's something more than that. It's easy to say it's the product too but that has always been good. It's something. There is something about us now that I can't quite grasp.

CEO stays silent, reflective

CEO: (*mumbles almost to self*) The people have found a meaning in what we do I think. (*Then louder*) You know I think the people are great and perhaps they think we are too. We are now learning in a better way. I'm sure of it.

(*Points finger at HR Manager*) I know you'll come up with these measures and knowing what I have learned about you they are going to be just what we need. If you want to mull over any ideas with me any time just let me know.

HR Manager: Thanks, I'm already writing it in my head as we speak

CEO: OK, well see you later. (*returns to work and then remembers*) Wait a moment, I've just remembered. There's something I've been working on privately. We may well make an acquisition. I'll give you the details and I'd like you to work on a briefing for all employees very, very quickly. If we don't the grapevine will beat us and I don't want that. Rumours are dangerous – well you know that don't you.

HR Manager: (*In surprise*) Acquisition? That's great news.

CEO: I'll send the papers to your office this afternoon. It would be good if you could let me have a plan by tomorrow afternoon. I don't want us to delay on this one.

HR Manager: Definitely! I'll have it ready.

Freeze

CEO awakes and looks at MC

MC: *Conventional wisdom (and Marcus Buckingham) says that Great Managers do four things superbly well – selects a person, sets expectations, motivates the person, develops the person. So how do you think you are doing?*

CEO: *(Thinking) Not so bad......I guess. We are doing well. But it's not me. My job, I believe is to set the framework and allow the professionals to do their job.*

MC: *And maybe you are doing just that. What if I were to tell you that all research shows that unless those principles are followed that companies and organisations gradually disintegrate. It's not a big crash no, but like a slow lingering death.*

CEO: *Is that true. Then I'm glad we are not like the others. I wouldn't let that happen. We've come too far to spoil it. (CEO fixes gaze on the audience and wags finger)*

MC: *Nods and CEO freezes.*

MC: *(To audience) What further picture is emerging now?*

MC Organises the discussion

MC: *A different picture is emerging. One where the CEO is aware of the necessity of people being involved, recognized and rewarded. He also is hot on communication. He will not allow the rumour machine to gain the upper hand.*

Now Let's now see what comments the Employees have on the way they are led.

Scene 6

Employee 2: So let's talk about how you are settling in? You've been here two months and from what I've seen you've listened and learned. And you were pretty good in the first place.

New Employee 1: *Smiles.* It has been better than I expected. People are not suspicious of you here and want you to do well. Everyone wants to help you succeed. It's amazing. I've made mistakes of course but there's no huge drama about it. We focus on what we learned from it and how it will not recur again. I like it.

Employee 2: Do you feel that you are needed here?

New Employee 1: Oh Yes! I feel part of a team and part of a family. Of course there is the odd difficult person here and there and nobody is ever going to find a cure for being moody now and then – we all get moody. This isn't heaven, it's human but most of all this company acts like a decent human being.

Employee 2: Nice way of putting it.

New Employee 1: Yeah deep down our managers.......they are all good people. They focus on bringing the best out of us not pointing out the little error made.

Employee 2: It wasn't always like this you know. It sort of evolved. I think that's the word. You could see greater care on recruitment, on onboarding, greater effort in ensuring that people know what is expected of them and heaps of praise and recognition. What used to tick us off was poor communication but now it's as if special effort is given to that.

New Employee 1: *(Considering what Employee has said)* Is that why you've stayed all this time?

Employee 2: *(Laughs and wags finger at employee)* I am and always will be optimistic about work here. Sales makes you optimistic don't you think? It's probably true I thought about leaving in the first year or so. I got plenty of better offers but then when things here changed for the better all that went away. There's no reason for me to leave. None at all.

New Employee 1: That makes me feel good to be here. *(Both smile and pause)*

Employee 2: *(Changing Subject)* Incidentally, have you heard about the acquisition

New Employee 1: *(In surprise)* No, I haven't.

Employee 2: *(With a wry smile)* You will tomorrow. They are briefing us. I glanced at some papers being sent to the HR Manager's office requesting the brief be prepared. But keep it between you and me ok.

New Employee 1: ok

Employee 2: Now is there anything else I can help you with during your probation. It won't stop there of course. You can get my help any time.

New Employee 1: I'm up to speed all on my targets now. I could do with smashing them completely like you do but other than that I think I'm ok.

Employee 2: Well let me do some more visits with you and I'll give you some guidance on what works for me and then we'll see what we need to adapt for you. How's that sound?

New Employee 1: Cool, thanks.

Scene Freezes

MC: *Addresses the audience. What is happening? Is this unusual ? Or is it the way things should be.*

Organises questions and continues

Let's go back now and see how the CEO and HR Manager are dealing with things:

Cut to CEO and HR Manager

Scene 7

CEO: Your predecessor was working on a new PDR form before you arrived. As I recollect the plan was it was to be introduced this coming quarter. Have you had time to review it?

HR Manager: *(Frowns)* Talking to people it seems the form has been changed a number of times and each time it has become more complex. It has surprised me because my predecessor did some very good things. You know don't you that any new form is useless. In fact every time a new HR Manager arrives they want to change the form. *(CEO's face looks interested).* But I'll let you into a secret. It will be useless. Performance Management is not about the form; it's about developing people to manage performance. Having said that I'd like to make the process much simpler so the Managers don't complain about HR complexity.

CEO: Ok, look I'm interested in the end results and not the means by which they are achieved. I'm no HR expert so I'll trust your judgement. I'm sure it will enable performance to improve rather than the opposite, right?

HR Manager: *(Laughing)* Of course. You'll see.

CEO: *(Thinking)* Incidentally a lot of the CEO's I talk to are introducing a new swipe card system for when employees arrive and leave. What do you think?

HR Manager considers

HR Manager: We would need to communicate this to employees and explain the reason. If we don't they will assume we don't trust them. Why are you thinking we should do it? I've always believed that it's people and not machines that encourage people to be at and stay at work.

CEO: And I agree with you also. One of the people I was talking to told a story about an employee trapped in a building when there was a fire and they did not know she was there. It scared me to be honest. I don't want anyone feeling that we don't trust them. What do you recommend?

HR Manager: Let's set up a group including some employees and find the best way of doing it or the best way of accounting for people on the premises at any given time. How does that sound?

CEO: *(sounding optimistic)* I like it. My only condition is that it does not drag out and fizzle away. Let's get the focus group or whatever completed within 6 weeks. Doable?

HR Manager: Yes, it is.

CEO: *(in a concluding tone)* Great. We'll meet in a month then to get an update on where we are on this one. By the way, how is your work coming along with the measures?

HR Manager: Good thanks. Give me another few days and I'll have something ready to present.

Both freeze and cuts to MC

MC: *(To audience) A fundamental issue for all employees is trust. To be honest in my lifetime I can think of no employee who's worked with me or alongside me who has said "You know what I'm really going to make a mess of it today". It doesn't happen. All of us arrive at work to do our best. However, just as with the teaching profession where arguably there are no bad students only bad teachers we can postulate that there are no bad employees only bad managers. Yes there are people with different sets of skills, knowledge and experience but the really great Manager works to bring out the best that all individuals have.*

The problem that I have with systems which check where people are is that although it can sound probable that a swipe card system is used for Health and Safety reasons in reality it never is. It's not words which count; it's the actions which take place following the words. So the swipe card system is introduced to "save lives" but oh….suddenly people get notes from "personnel" asking them to explain why they were 7.5 minutes late for work etc etc.

And you see I used the word "personnel" deliberately. Forgive me if you disagree with me but arguably the role of personnel is to catch people doing things wrong whereas the role of HR is to catch people doing things right. Has a different ring to it doesn't it?

And that's all about trust. You see the swipecard system to a highly intelligent worker means "oh, you only want to start thinking when I swipe in at 8.30 and swipe out at 5.30 or whatever. You don't want me to think for you outside those hours so have it your way, I won't."

And when you have time also think of the subliminal message which is being sent to all employees through the concept of "Compensation and Benefits" – terms which I have stayed away from throughout my career.

(MC Encourages debate from the audience)

Now let's see a section of the review between the Sales Manager and the new employee.

Cuts to meeting

Scene 8

Sales Manager: *(Smiling)* Well as you know you passed your probation and with ease to be honest. We are glad that you are here. Congratulations!

Employee 1: Thanks. It did not seem difficult to be honest. Everyone here is rooting for you to do well. I got great help from you and also from *(Employee 2 name)*. He/She was very, very helpful.

Sales Manager: Yes, ever since we introduced that buddy system things have improved greatly and *(Employee 2 name)* is one of the best we have in helping people settle in. I'll see her also to thank her. *(Changes subject)* Ok, so now that we are through probation I'd like you to write your own targets for this coming quarter and the two beyond. Once you've done that we can go through and discuss. Don't make them too tough but make them stretching. Let's agree what we would both regard as meeting performance requirements and what would be classed as "exceeding expectations". How does that sound to you?

Employee 1; Yes, I really like that approach. I'll write them today and bring to you tomorrow.

Sales Manager: Great! That means you are beginning with an Exceed Expectations !! Just one other thing. You know that contract you won with DEF company? *(Employee nods)* It was unusual as we've tried a while and I know you have a contact there but I think the technique you may have used could be interesting for us. Do you mind if I ask *(Employee 2 name)* to observe the techniques you are using and reports back to me on it – and you as well? I know he/she's visiting with you soon.

Employee 1: *(Feeling proud)* Yes, sure. I'll be really happy to be part of that. Thank you. And I'll be ready with my targets tomorrow.

Cuts to MC. Some weeks have passed by

MC: We are having different types of conversations now. Two months have passed so let's now look in on the conversation between the two Employees.

Cuts to conversation with employees.

Scene 9

Employee 2: So all going well? You are more or less flying solo now and the way you are flying. Wow!! That exercise we did on your technique was useful too.

New Employee 1: Well it was you that noticed that. I didn't even realize I was doing it.

Employee 2: Sometimes we don't notice our own techniques. It takes an observer to spot it. And you are really good at it.

New Employee 1: *(Sounding a little hesitant)* HR wants me to do a few role plays on it and give advice. I said I would if you'd help. Is that ok?

Employee 2: *(Laughs)* Of course it is You know you can hear them say here "People are our most important resource". Well here they are not perfect but in fairness they try. That's what I like about it. *(Pauses)* Hey did I tell you about my son.

New Employee 1: Yes, I heard about it. But tell me more

Employee 2: Well this is what happened. He needed to go into hospital for a while and I wanted to change my hours so I could visit. They wanted to give me emergency leave for a few days but I said the adjusted hours would do it and they agreed. They found out his age and where he was and sent a gift to the hospital with a note for me and my husband/wife also.

New Employee 1: They care don't they.

Employee 2: I'll say. It comes at a time when I've been made a big offer to leave and with promotion to Manager within a year but I'm not going. I turned it down.

New Employee 1: Really???

Employee 2: Yup, turned it down. I know I'll get promotion here soon. The important thing is that the company did something for me and I felt that trust in me deserved that response. I start shadowing *(Sales Manager name)* from next month and I'll commence the Leadership programme also.

New Employee 1: *(pleases)* Wow! I'll need to start calling you Boss!! You are the best in this Department for sure. *(Softly and genuinely)* I'm glad you are staying. It wouldn't be the same without you.

Employee 2: Thanks. I hope I'm here for years.

Both are lost in thought as the CEO enters.

CEO: Aha! Thinking of new ideas for us, that's great. This is exactly the thing we need. You see I always say that our employees are our best resource.

(if audience laughs or applauds the CEO turns to the audience in perplexity)

CEO: So how are things? How are you doing? We are doing well you know and you guys are helping us a lot. *(With sincerity)* Thank you! Thank you so much!

Employees: *(Both speak together. They are pleased to see the CEO. This time words and body language coincide)* Yes all is fine, thank you. It's good. Enjoying the work. Good to see you.

CEO: Excellent. Look I'm having a breakfast meeting with a cross section of employees next week to get some ideas and feedback. Can I ask you both to come.?

Both: *(They nod)* Yes, Yes that will be great. Thank you.

CEO: OK, I'll arrange it. Bye guys – and thanks again

(Walks away with self satisfied smile)

Freeze and cut to MC:

MC: *(Addresses Audience)* What has changed? Are the changes major? Are they possible or is this a fantasy world?

MC organizes discussion with audience

MC: *Continues*

You don't feel there is a sign of disengagement now, do you. When there is you know it and when there isn't you know it too. But all too often we ignore the signs I listed in the first part of this workshop.

These people are approaching the status of "raving fans". But why?

Let's now go back to a conversation between the CEO and the HR Manager

Scene 10

CEO: There's a great spirit developing. I can feel it. Can you?

HR Manager: Yes, I can

CEO: We are doing the right things, aren't we? I always knew that if we focused on people results would come. And they are much better than I was expecting

HR Manager *(Smiles)* They really are. And there's something else. You know *(Employee 2 name)* was offered a new position elsewhere with a package much greater than ours and promotion.

CEO: What! I saw him/her the other day and he/she seemed fine. She was with *(Employee 1 mname)* – the new sales employee. Is he/she going to resign?

HR Manager: *(Laughs)* No. He/She just came to let me know in case word got out. He/She's a very good employee. We had already arranged job shadowing and for him/her to be on the Leadership Development programme. What I'm saying is that we are reaching a level of engagement which will enable us to keep employees. And I like that!

CEO: *(mutters almost to self)* That is such good news

HR Manager: It's the way that everybody at senior level acts towards employees.

CEO: *(Questioning)* Do you really think so. Honestly?

HR Manager: *(makes as if to speak but stops)*

Scene freezes. HR Manager stands and looks at audience and MC.

HR Manager: You know I had a nightmare once that I was in this position before except then it was a well meaning environment but things were going wrong. I didn't have the answers to back up my feelings – to back up my opinion. In my dream I had no answers because I had no evidence. I just had my feelings. My intuition. And I couldn't back it up??

I've been working hard on a framework. You know I don't want HR to be annoying. I don't want other departments or even us slaving over extracting data which takes for ever and is then meaningless. But I do believe there is data that can help us and I know where to get it. And we will be able to measure continuously and link back to our overall business performance.

How does that sound to you?

MC: Well it sounds like heaven to be honest. What are you going to do now.?

HR Manager: I'm going to explain it all to the CEO

MC: Ok, then lets's wake him/her up

MC waves a hand to unfreeze CEO

CEO : So where was I?

HR Manager: You were wondering why everything is going so well and how we can know.

CEO: Yes, and you were going to come up with some answers.

HR Manager: Yes, I think I can. I'd like to give you and the management team a presentation tomorrow at our team meeting.

CEO: Tomorrow?

HR Manager: I know its short notice but do you think I can.

CEO: (Smiling) Of course. This is important. You'll have an hour at the start of the meeting. I'm looking forward to it.

Freeze

MC: *Ok well before we hear the HR Manager's presentation let's break into groups and consider no more than 12 measures which you would use to measure the areas for which HR should take primary responsibility.*

We can then take a look at what you have as groups and what the HR Manager has selected. Now let's be clear on this: as much as we aim for objectivity every one of us will retain a personal measure because......well we like it. And that's fine. Equally what the HR manager will present is a core set of measures there may be others which are necessary for each specific company or organization. This is because all environments differ and the maturity levels of organisations differ also .

(Groups are organized)

Break

5 ACT THREE

MC: *Thank you everybody for the hard work you have put into the sessions and for patient listening to the drama as it has unfolded. My observation over the years is that put a Consultant or a trainer in front of an audience and attention starts to drift fairly quickly. Yet when a story is told dramatically we are keen to learn what happens next.*

This is the first time that we have tried it this way and I believe that we can deal with many HR and Leadership issues in this way generally and for specific companies who wish to highlight issues. You may be inspired now to write your own. Personally, I believe we understand and learn in a better way when we do. Remember the old Chinese proverb:

I hear and I forget

I see and I remember

I Do and I understand.

Ok, well we left maybe a slightly nervous or perhaps very confident HR Manager arranging to come in and deliver a presentation to the management team on HR measures. In the preparation for this I have drawn on the work of David Ulrich, Marcus Buckingham, Jac Fitz-Enz, John Kotter, Gareth Jones and Rob Goffee, Linda Holbeche and John Boudreau.

The moment has arrived. Can you imagine what he/she is feeling like. Rehearsing most of the evening and has gone to bed at a good hour but cannot sleep. The detail of the presentation and how he/she is going to deliver it is going through his/her mind.

Sometimes he/she sees him/herself losing his/her way and the management team look uninspired. Sometimes he/she is totally fluent and sees the admiring faces of the team. That's how we play it out isn't it before a major event and this is a major event for the HR Manager.

So let us move to the meeting room and join the meeting. It's about to begin.

Cuts to meeting room

MC: *(Continues)* *You know the CEO, the HR Manager and the Sales Manager and they have been joined by the Finance Manager and the Operations Manager.*

Let's join the meeting which is about to start:

We join as general chatter is under way. The CEO brings meeting to order.

CEO: Ok, ok. Thanks. You saw yesterday that I changed the agenda to allow HR Manager to deliver a presentation to us on the way we should measure Human Resources. *(HR Manager name)*, over to you.

HR Manager: Thank you CEO. *(Addresses the group and the audience).* HR is always in a difficult place isn't it. I've heard some people – not here of course – describe us as a necessary evil, part of the fat overhead or just a downright nuisance.

(Some amused looks from those gathered)

HR Manager: *(Continues)* I know. I don't blame you. I think we have failed you in showing that we are a true profession which adds value to the organization. We live in the shadows and you have your opinion of our value. It's our fault that we have not provided worthwhile measures

You can *(Nods to the Sales manager)* Achieving sales targets and building our revenue is our lifeblood

You *(Nods to operations)* have productivity ratios, customer service percentages, shift targets etc . You have responsibility for the quality of the operation

And you *(Nods to the Finance manager)* have the most well established and universal financial targets of all. You are responsible for the financial health of the company

And yet we all acknowledge don't we that people are our greatest asset? Yet we don't really have the same kind of rigorous measures for HR that we do in the other disciplines. No wonder you think we are an irrelevancy. *(Smiles)*

I'm going to recommend a number of measures we should adopt to demonstrate a clear link between people practices and overall performance. If we don't get these right then my belief is that overall performance will suffer.

So let's begin:

(Pauses and says) Yes I know, you can't wait.

I have organized the measures in no priority order I have to say but like this:

We have:

1 No of Staff in Post and vacant positions open for no more than x weeks

(The target appears on bullet point for audience to see as with all)

Ops Manager: What do you mean by that?

HR Manager: There's a lot behind it. In a perfect world the answer would be 100% full and 0

vacancies at all times because we are magnificent at Manpower Planning.

(Group chuckles)

(Continues) I want to spend more time with you looking at the likely vacancies for the year ahead that arise through growth and planning well in advance to fill them. If we are taken aback by an unforeseen vacancy I'd like to agree with you a target number of weeks for filling. Obviously, it's easier to fill a labour vacancy than an executive so it would be useful to agree a small number of targets for each level.

Ops Manager/Finance Manager: Good idea

HR Manager: For my second target I'd like to propose:

2   Revenue and profit per employee.

Finance Manager: OK, I like that but how will you make it meaningful. Just taken as a number it won't help us.

HR Manager: I agree. We need to assess the industry average and benchmark ourselves against the competition. Our products and services won't be competitive unless our costs are controlled. Once we have the benchmark we can work on where we may have inflated costs compared to others.

Ops Manager/Sales Manager/Finance Manager: We can help you/ I have some data/ Lets form a group to look at this/ I think it will help us.

HR Manager: I agree this is just the start. Once we've agreed on the parameters and the targets I suggest we meet as a group to agree all details.

Pauses and then continue)

My third target deals with labour turnover and retention/stability index. It costs a lot of money to replace someone and also there is the hidden cost which arises from the effect on people around the departing employee and we can lose knowledge dramatically. Now I'm not saying that we don't need an injection of new blood from time to time but senseless hiring of staff is a drain on resources. To be honest I think here it's an area where we are pretty good. So the target will be:

3   Labour turnover rate which is calculated like this :

Total number of leavers over period   x 100

Average total number employed over period

And retention/stability

Number of staff with service of one year or more   x 100

Total number of staff in post one year or more

Ops Manager: Why do we need both?

HR Manager: Good question. If we do have a turnover problem it helps us pinpoint if it's with new starters – and if it is then we may have an onboarding problem. And if it is more experienced employees then we will need to investigate the cause. The point is we have primary data to point us in the right direction.

(Nods from around the table)

HR Manager: *(Continues)* My fourth measure is:

4   The % of employees achieving objectives

CEO: What's the thinking behind that one ?

HR Manager: Well the closer we are to 100% the more likely the overall business plan has been achieved. If people are not achieving objectives then we are doing something wrong. It's a broad measure but if we drill down afterwards we will find issues such as motivation, reward, succession planning, development, communication and so on. Or maybe we have capability issues. The thing is do we know this minute how close all people are to achieving their objectives?

(Room goes silent and people look away)

CEO: No, the truth is we don't. We've never measured it like that before. *(Thinking)* It makes a lot of sense.

HR Manager: Good – and it links in with the fifth measure which is competence. Therefore the measure is:

5   Percentage of employees with full competence level

Now what does that mean? For those who manage and lead people we will have the competences from our Leadership model plus the technical know how required to carry out the job. Therefore, we will have defined how well they lead and manage based on the following:

0 – No competence and perhaps toxic behaviour

1 – Some Competence

2 – Acceptable competence

3 – Complete mastery

I don't want to prejudge the number of leadership competences or technical know how competences. We need to establish this as a group and maybe seek the guidance of an external Consultant to help us.

Finance Manager: We can't do it internally?

Sales Manager: I like the idea of external help. The Consultant will see things that we may miss.

(The group nods)

(HR manager pauses and continues)

My sixth measure deals with how well employees are engaged. So simply put:

6   The engagement rate of employees

Operations Manager: I've heard about this but what does it mean exactly. Like employee satisfaction?

HR Manager: It is in a way but it's not employee satisfaction. It measures the willingness of people to go the extra mile or as they say to give discretionary effort. Actually, my observation is that here engagement levels are quite good – but we don't know because we don't measure it. The other thing is that this might be one measure but the actions required deriving from the questions will mean we have a lot to do.

CEO: What kind of questions are asked?

HR Manager: There are forty five questions actually but there are twelve which provide the solid foundation on which to build success and which are linked to high performance

Finance Manager: *(Curious)* What are they as a matter of interest?

HR Manager: They are:

1 Do I know what is expected of me at work?

2 Do I have the materials and equipment I need to do my work right?

3 At work do I have the opportunity to do what I do best every day?

4 In the last seven days have I received recognition or praise for good work?

5 Does my supervisor, or someone at work, seem to care about me as a person?

6 Is there someone at work who encourages my development?

7 At work do my opinions seem to count?

8 Does the mission/purpose of my company make me feel like my work is important?

9 Are my co-workers committed to doing quality work?

10 Do I have a best friend at work?

11 In the last six months have I talked with someone about my progress?

12 At work have I had opportunities to learn and grow?

If we get top marks for these we are on our way to achieving high performance. The documented evidence between high performance and high engagement is well known.

Ops Director: What does that mean?

HR Manager: We will achieve results much higher than the industry average.

(Has their interest)

(Continues)

There is one measure from the Engagement Survey we take out and use as stand alone. It is fundamental to success.

Sales Manager: Which one

HR Manager: The seventh measure is:

7   Manager satisfaction index

I'm not telling you anything you don't know when I tell you that people don't leave companies they leave Managers. Individual Managers have a high responsibility for the recruitment, objective setting and motivation of employees. They get it wrong and it can be disastrous. We need Managers to understand what is required and ensure they deliver on it.

Sales Manager: What if someone gets great results but is a poor leader?

CEO: Let me answer that. If it's development that's required we'll give it. If we've put a square peg in a round hole we'll redeploy. If it's behaviour that they refuse to change and contravenes our values then it will be a diplomatic and respectful CDE.

Finance Manager: Uh?? CDE?

CEO: *(briskly)* Career Development......Elsewhere!

HR Manager: *(Smiling)* Thank you. Before I move onto my next measure there is another question which I intend to use which experts say is also indicative of high performance. It is known as the eNPS question. Anyone know what that is?

All: *(Shake heads, mutter no)*

OK well I will come back to it. Let's move on to my next measure – the eighth:

8   No of Innovations leading to reduction in cost or increase in profit

By now the level of trust and engagement in the company will be high. Employees will be willing to take risks and make bold suggestions. They will not be playing it safe. They will want to innovate. We will be able to calculate the value of the innovations either through reduced cost or increased profit.

CEO: *(Thinking out loud)* We should create an award or something to encourage it. Sorry just thinking. Please continue.

HR Manager: My ninth measure deals with the hire of managers or not !

9   The ratio of internal promotion to external hire

Again all the research shows that internal promotees do better than external hires because they know the culture – the way it's done round here. If we've developed them well they can hit the ground running. This is not to say we shouldn't hire from outside but I would prefer to see a 70-30 or 80-20 ratio in favour of internal selections.

I'm going to stick my neck out here too. I think we should promote on potential not on the ability to do the job.

Finance Manager: You'd better explain that one *(others mumble agreement)*

HR Manager: We tend to wait until someone is ready for the job but when they go into it's too late. Put someone in who has high potential and can only do 70-80% you watch them rise to the challenge to get there – and the innovation? Well, I think you'll be making a few awards (*smiles*

at CEO). When we wait until they can do the job we allow them to coast and just wait for the next senior opportunity. We should also keep people on the edge of a challenge.

Ops Manager: (Musing) On the edge of a challenge.

HR Manager: My tenth measure supports this last one:

10 Number of key positions with identified successors

This speaks for itself. We need to agree the jobs which are so important that they need a developed successor so that movement leads to automatic replacement. For this we may need a change of culture. All too often we can find people hiring those who are controllable, less talented than they are because they fear losing their job. It's a false logic because they will lose it with that tactic anyway as the company becomes a company of dwarves and lesser than the competition.

CEO: You know I'm going to make that a substantial objective for Managers with a high reward if they do it.

Finance Manager: It's a great idea. Just one comment I have is this: if the first manager who trains a superior successor is axed you'll see that objective wither.

CEO: I agree, we will need to ensure that does not happen. *(Turning to HR Manager)* Are there other meaures you'd like to propose?

HR Manager: I have left it at 10 but I'm open to two further measures to be added which the team might like. I thought that might emerge now after my presentation or when we get into detailed meeting.

CEO: Ok, thank you HR Manager. You've given us a lot to consider. Team, can I have your views on the measures.

But wait *(HR Manager name)* what was that eNPS question you were going to tell us about?

Freeze

6 ACT FOUR - CLOSING

MC: *We'll leave them now as their debate will continue but if you were part of that team and wanting to comment to the CEO what would you be saying? And do you know what the eNPS question is?*

Also what additional measures do you think are critical to be brought out? Remember some may be embedded in the overall measure so that you can't reach it without achieving a subordinate measure.

The Floor is open to questions. (MC wonders if they will consider eNPS as the 11th measure)

(MC organizes questions)

MC: *OK thank you based on your comments the final list of measures now looks like this. (MC goes through the bullet pointed list of 10 measures plus two proposed by audience.*

The eNPS question is of course "On a scale of 1-10 how likely are you to recommend this organization to a friend as a great place to work?"

For all of us here today I would like to close with the following observations:

1 There are many things HR professionals need to know but underpinning what we are doing today is a thorough understanding of how to connect people to the company and a strong understanding of how developing capabilities can enable that. Without this HR will be well meaning and will act with good intent but are likely to make bad judgement calls.

2 HR needs a sound understanding also of all HR practices. David Ulrich provides four groupings:

a) *Flow of People. What happens to this key asset? How is the talent managed as it comes in and flows through the organization?*

b) *Flow of Performance Management. Defining the standards and measures and ensuring there is accountability in reaching those standards. The reward for achieving should be well defined and the penalties for not.*

c) *Flow of Information. Attention is paid to ensuring that people know what is happening and why. Information needs to be two-way.*

d) *Flow of work. It needs to be clear who does the work, how and where it is done and how individual efforts aggregate into teamwork.*

3 HR Professionals need to understand where the importance lies for HR effectiveness and influence on business performance. Research at the University of Michigan's Business School has shown that the greatest impact on Business performance comes with greater Strategic Contribution and personal credibility. We need to work on these.

4 Everyone involved in the running of a company or organization must understand the requirements of customers, investors, the market, emerging technologies. After that they must be able to translate this understanding into the necessary employee behaviours and capabilities. If that cannot be done the organization will have difficulty staying alive. As Goffee and Jones say as leaders we need "to instill our organisations with meaning."

I have some last thoughts for you before we close. Ask yourself this question: "List four people whose career you have made better?" How quickly are you able to do that?

To paraphrase Goffee and Jones ""As leaders we need to create a compelling narrative. We must find a way of looking at the world which allows others not only to understand their role in it but also to be excited by it. Arguably, the four elements which employees want from their leaders are authenticity, significance, excitement and a sense of community." As leaders we need to capture the attention of our employees and motivate people to follow our way —our vision and our dreams.

Lastly, I have a quote from Studs Terkel's book "Working": "Work is about daily meaning as well as daily bread; for recognition as well as cash; in short for a sort of life rather than a Monday-Friday sort of dying....We have a right to ask of work that it include meaning, recognition, astonishment and life."

Facilitator gives a final summing up of the workshop. Calls forward actors for tribute and mentions all who took part in administration and production.

CLOSE

7 APPENDIX - WORKBOOK

LIVING IN THE DARK SHADOW OF OPINION

Workbook

This workbook is for you to record your observations and thoughts as the dramatic workshop progresses.

Act 1 Scene 1 and Scene 2

Here we see a sales candidate being offered and accepting a job from the Sales Manager and a very new HR Manager is just having a first conversation with the CEO following acceptance.

What do you notice about both new hires? What has happened in the conversation between the HR Manager and the CEO?

Act 1 Scene 3

This scene details the conversation between the new hire and an existing employee. We also see a meeting between the new Sales employee and the Sales Manager. What do the conversations tell you about the company? Does this type of conversation exist in your company? What actions can we take to improve the situation?

Act 1 Scene 4

This shows a meeting between the CEO, HR Manager and Sales Manager to discuss the performance of the new hire. What does it tell you about onboarding of new hires and the performance management process. Does this happen at your organization? What would you do to improve the situation?

Act 1 Scene 5

This scene details a conversation between the CEO and the HR Manager. What are we now learning about this organization as a result of the CEO comments. Is he right to hide the details of the acquisition?

Act 1 Scene 6

In this scene we see another conversation between the two employees. Do upper management really know what they are thinking and feeling? Do you know what your own employees are thinking and feeling?

Act 1 Scene 7

This scene details a conversation between the CEO and HR Manager. It covers the issue of a new performance management form and the introduction of an attendance swipe card system. What further conclusions can we draw on the way things are progressing? What are your views on the CEO so far? Is the HR Manager managing the situation?

Act 1 Scene 8

We see a short scene between the Sales Manager and the new hire. What does the conversation tell you about the Sales Manager. How could it be improved?

Act 1 Scene 9

We return to a conversation between the two employees. An incident has arisen which has disaffected the long serving employee. How does the handling of the incident impact on the long serving employee and the new employee. Do we allow issues like this to arise in our organisations? How do we perceive the arrival of the CEO on the scene?

Act 1 Scene 10

This scene shows you a meeting of the management team. What do we learn from this about the team and the general attitude of the company?

Intermission

Summarise here the things you would do differently in that organization to improve performance and engagement. Ask yourself the question: "In my own organization do we do the things I am recommending right now?"

Act 2

Act 2 should show a different picture in the way situations in an organization are managed. As you watch the scenes develop note down for your own use practices you see and which you might adopt in your organization. Are there other things you do which are better? What are they?

Act 3

Act III is primarily a presentation from the HR Manager to the Leadership Team on how HR performance should be measured in the future. Does it cover the essential items? Are there any points you would like to see included as measures? What will you take away as a result of this presentation?

8 ABOUT THE AUTHOR

 Maurice Collis has substantial experience in the area of HR practicalities and Leadership and particularly in People Development and HR metrics. He has over 35 years of experience in HR and a deep knowledge of the MENA region. He is a Fellow of the CIPD and holds a BA, Diploma in Management Studies as well as an MBA. He has held positions at Director, GM and MD level.

He came first to the Region in 1998 in senior HR roles for Agility and NREC in Kuwait and went on to provide management development and personnel services to Kuwaiti organizations through the creation of HRD International.

Whilst working with NREC, Kuwait he established the Kuwait Maastricht Business School which has more than 400 MBA students annually.

In 2004 he came to Lebanon to establish and manage businesses for his previous Kuwaiti company using his HR skills to recruit the required teams. His most recent employed position was at averda whom he joined in October 2009 as Corporate HR Director. In this position as throughout his career he aimed for simple solutions which aided rather than hindered operational teams and revenue generators. He is highly knowledgeable in the essentials of HR operations, policies and procedures, recruitment and talent management and the techniques of employee engagement. Additionally he is a skilled facilitator and develops and runs a range of workshops for CEO's, Directors and Managers. He coaches and advises senior managers in leadership essentials and enables them to develop their skills to the full. He sees HR as a unit which must support the activities of the business and enable objectives to be achieved rather than getting in the way. He believes that HR is often the application of applied practical common sense and that this should be the driver for HR performance.

From a historical perspective, he obtained his first HR directorship in 1986 for the Royal Mail at Cardiff UK and then at Birmingham UK, where he oversaw all aspects of HR and industrial relations for their 5,500 employees. In 1996 he established his own management development and training consultancy with a focus on HR, Management Development, Leadership and organizational development consultancy services to major UK companies.

He has written articles on leadership and is at work on a book focusing on its ethical aspects. 'In recruiting people,' he says, 'I believe that character carries as much weight as skill.' He is also a writer of novels and short stories.

He lives in Lebanon with his wife and two young children and travels extensively on HR Business throughout the region.

He became a Consultant from 1 September 2013 and as of 1 October 2013 he is a Board Member for HRworks based in Beirut. More recently from January 2014 he has become a subject matter expert in HR for Deloitte in the UAE as well as a guest lecturer in HR at the American University of Beirut.

www.ingramcontent.com/pod-product-compliance
Lightning Source LLC
Chambersburg PA
CBHW071632170526
45166CB00003B/1296